Ernest Hawkins

Recent Expansion of the Church of England

The Ramsden Sermon for 1864, preached before the University of Oxford,

on Trinity Sunday

Ernest Hawkins

Recent Expansion of the Church of England
The Ramsden Sermon for 1864, preached before the University of Oxford, on Trinity Sunday

ISBN/EAN: 9783337088057

Printed in Europe, USA, Canada, Australia, Japan

Cover: Foto ©Lupo / pixelio.de

More available books at **www.hansebooks.com**

THE

RAMSDEN SERMON

FOR 1864,

EACHED BEFORE THE UNIVERSITY OF OXFORD,

ON TRINITY SUNDAY.

BY

ERNEST HAWKINS, B.D.

LATE FELLOW OF EXETER COLLEGE.

WITH AN APPENDIX OF DATES AND STATISTICS.

LONDON:

BELL AND DALDY, 186, FLEET STREET.

J. H. & J. PARKER, OXFORD AND LONDON.

1864.

TO

THE PRESIDENT, VICE-PRESIDENTS,

COMMITTEE,

AND OTHER MEMBERS

OF THE

Society for the Propagation of the Gospel,

THE FOLLOWING SERMON

IS RESPECTFULLY AND GRATEFULLY DEDICATED

BY THEIR OLD AND DEVOTED SERVANT,

THE AUTHOR.

RAMSDEN SERMON,

1864.

ACTS I. 8.

" Ye shall be witnesses unto me both in Jerusalem, and in all Judæa, and in Samaria, and unto the uttermost part of the earth."

SUCH was the wonderful announcement made by the risen Saviour to His Apostles on the Mount of Ascension. To them at the time, and for ten days afterwards, those parting words must have been truly a dark saying. Its meaning was first unfolded to them on the Day of Pentecost. The cloven tongues which then sat upon the head of each, and the marvellous gift thus instantaneously conferred, must have been to them a manifest token of the part which they were to take in the fulfilment of their Lord's promise. If they were to be His witnesses in all lands, they had the most convincing assurance that they would be enabled to deliver their testimony. For already the peasants and fishermen of Galilee had openly,

B

before strangers of every race and language, exercised their new gift. They had, in point of fact, been made witnesses to their Lord—to His resurrection—to His ascension—before multitudes of "men out of every nation under heaven," proclaiming in the language of each "the wonderful works of God."

Let us, then, consider what the *Commission* was that the twelve Apostles were called and empowered to execute. It was in its terms the most comprehensive, and in its object the most important, that had ever been confided to human agents. The charge given to them was nothing less than to bear the message of the Gospel to the whole world. "Ye shall be witnesses unto Me " both in Jerusalem, and in all Judæa, and in " Samaria, and unto the uttermost part of the " earth."

In these ever-memorable words we have clearly set forth, not only the *extent* to which the commission ran, but the *order* in which it was to be executed. God, in His own wise counsels, had made choice of a single nation—the family of Abraham—to be the depository of His truth, and the guardian of His law. To the Israelites belonged "the adoption, and the covenants, and the promises."[1] To them first, as a *nation*, was revealed the knowledge of the One living and true God ; and

[1] Rom. ix. 4.

from among their tribes, in the fulness of time, was to arise the Messiah, of whom Moses and the prophets spake—the Seed of Abraham, in whom all the families of the earth should be blessed—the Son of David, who should establish a universal kingdom, and reign for ever and ever. And thus, as God in His inscrutable wisdom had, for well-nigh two thousand years, confined the revelation of His will to the people of Israel, as to them alone of all the nations of the earth He had sent His priests, and messengers, and prophets; so, when a fuller revelation was to be made, and a better covenant established, this new dispensation was to be made known to the Jew before all others. During the season of His own earthly ministry, indeed, our Blessed Lord had said, " I am not sent, but unto the lost sheep of the house of Israel;"[1] and in His mysterious conversation with the two disciples, on their way to Emmaus, the very day of His resurrection, He declared it to be in the order of the Divine decrees that " Repentance " and remission of sins should be preached in His " name among all nations, *beginning at Jerusalem.*"[2] Twice, therefore, in the plainest and most emphatic manner—once in the words just cited, and then again at the very moment of His ascension— did our Lord, "to whom all power in heaven and in earth was given," leave it in charge to the

[1] Matt. xv. 24, and cf. Matt. x. 6.　　[2] Luke xxiv. 47.

Apostles to preach His Gospel everywhere, but to preach it first to the Jews.

How, and to what extent that great commission has been fulfilled, it is the province of ecclesiastical history to show. The Acts of the Apostles, indeed, record the bold and successful testimony which St. Peter and St. John delivered to the priests and people in the Temple, and in the streets of Jerusalem. We are told, too, as the result of their faithful preaching, that "the word "of God increased; and the number of the dis- "ciples multiplied in Jerusalem greatly, and a "great company of the priests were obedient to "the faith."[1]   Well, therefore, had the Lord's command been obeyed in the preaching of "re- pentance and remission of sins" in His name *first* at Jerusalem. But when, and by what means was the second, but far more important, part of His commission fulfilled?

The extension of the true Kingdom of the Messiah, as it began now to be understood, was brought about, in the first instance, in a way plainly providential. The rapid triumphs of the new Faith in the Holy City were too much for the jealous tempers and deep-seated prejudices of the Priests and Scribes. They had failed to silence the Apostles by stripes and imprisonment. They seemed resolved to persecute them to the death,

[1] Acts vi. 7.

and to deal with the servants as they had dealt with their Lord. St. Stephen was the first to seal his testimony with his blood; and so successfully had the passions of the people been excited, that, as we read, " there was a great persecution against " the Church that was at Jerusalem, and they " were all scattered abroad throughout the regions " of Judæa and Samaria . . . and they that were " scattered abroad went everywhere preaching " the word." [1] The Apostles, indeed, remained for a time at the post of danger, but, as soon as they heard that Samaria had received the word of God, they sent Peter and John to impart to them the gift of the Holy Ghost. Thus, then, was the command of the Lord observed, in the witness which was given to Him in Jerusalem, and "in all Judæa, and in Samaria."

How the glad tidings were carried forward from city to city, especially by the persecutor-convert, St. Paul, it would be beyond my present subject to relate. Before, however, that great ambassador of Christ had finished his course, he had carried the Gospel to the Jew first, and then to the Gentile, through the chief towns of Asia Minor, Macedonia, and Greece—nay, he had carried it to imperial Rome, and made it known even in the household of Cæsar. By St. Peter, and others of the Holy Brotherhood, it was published in Cappadocia,

[1] Acts viii. 1, 4.

Pontus, and Bithynia, in Assyria, Ethiopia, and Egypt. So that it may be said, without exaggeration, that there was hardly a country of the then known world where the voice of the witnesses of Christ had not been heard. " Their sound had gone out into all lands, and their words into the ends of the world." [1]

It would be interesting to trace the gradual triumphs of the Gospel in the early and the mediæval ages, but time and space forbid the attempt. I must come down at once to modern times. My especial subject on this day is not the growth and spread of the Church universal, but " the extension of the Church of England " over the colonies and dependencies of the " British empire " [A]—a subject limited, indeed, but still one of prodigious reach and extent. What, then, is the territory comprised within the colonies and dependencies of Great Britain ? Not less than *a sixth part* of the entire surface of the earth. And what is the total population of that subject empire with which the Missionaries of our Church have by a more special obligation to deal? It is, indeed, a vast multitude which defies any very precise reckoning, but is set down by the best authorities at little short of 200,000,000, or about *one-fifth* of the

[1] Psalm xix. 4.
[A] The *Letters* throughout refer to the *Appendix*.

inhabitants of the world.[B] Now, brethren, the first and appalling thought suggested by these facts is, that the great bulk of the people with whom we are thus brought into a Providential relation are *heathen* still, living and dying without even the faintest knowledge of Christ or His law. By a marvellous dispensation of the Divine Will, one of the largest, most populous, and most civilized divisions of the eastern world has been committed to our trust. We have in the vast Peninsula of India the guardianship and government of many nations of various origin, and speaking different languages. They are subject to our sovereign; their laws are administered by magistrates sent out from this country; an enormous revenue is raised from their land and their industry; nor can it be doubted that the wealth, power, and political influence of Great Britain are largely increased by her connexion with India. The foundations of our empire there were laid more than a century ago. [C] What then, from a religious point of view, has been the result of this long intercourse of Christian conquerors with a subject heathen people? While a former invasion has left its permanent mark upon the country, not only in solid and magnificent mosques, but in many millions of converts to the faith of the victorious Mussulman, somewhere about sixty or seventy thousand native

Christians make up the whole number that the
united exertions of both of our great Missionary
Societies have, up to the present time, been
enabled to gather into the fold of Christ. This,
indeed, is not the whole, nor nearly the whole,
number of those who have been converted to
Christianity, in one form or other; but I confine
myself, as my subject confines me, to the operations and extension of the Church of England.[D]
Let us trust, however, as we well may, that the
progress of the Gospel in heathen India for the
past century is no measure of the advance which,
under God's blessing, it is likely to make for the
time to come. Just fifty years ago, under protest
from many distinguished men, and with very real
apprehensions of the results which might follow
a measure, in their view, so rash and quixotic, a
single bishop was (though almost surreptitiously)
introduced into India.[E]   More than twenty years
afterwards, the experiment having proved a safe
one, a second and a third were added, making, in
all, one for each of the Presidencies. Since that
date province after province has been annexed
to the Central Government; but, except that the
Bishop of Madras has been relieved of the spiritual
oversight of CEYLON, by the erection of the See of
Colombo, in 1845, the organization of the Church
has remained as it was then fixed.

At this moment the Bishop of Calcutta presides

over a diocese which stretches over thirty-three degrees of latitude and sixteen of longitude, which is inhabited by nations speaking many different languages, and which it requires four years at the least to visit. These being the bare facts of the case, are we not constrained to ask whether, if it were right to send a bishop to Calcutta at all, it is not the very climax of unreason to leave him sole spiritual overseer of so enormous a territory—a territory extending from the Irawaddy to the Indus, and from Peshawur to Singapore? Surely such a glaring disproportion between the duty imposed, and the means of discharging it, cannot be much longer permitted to continue.[F] A fuller sense of Christian obligation on the part of the public, and a wiser and more enlightened principle of government on the part of the rulers of that great empire, must surely ere long lead to some great extension and improvement of its ecclesiastical organization. Recent experience has abundantly proved that the danger to British supremacy did not arise, as so often faithlessly predicted, from the introduction of Christianity; for when, seven years ago, the great bulk of the Hindoo and Mussulman populations were leagued together against the rule of the foreigner, the native Christians to a man stood true.

The empire of India has been committed by God to the keeping of a Christian people. Away, then

with the infidel thought that He will suffer us to
be dispossessed of the land, if we venture to impart
a knowledge of His law, and the truths of His
salvation, to its millions of heathen idolaters.
Should we not rather feel that as we hold that
vast dependency in trust for *Him*, we shall hold
it only so long as we give proof of an earnest
desire to honour His name among the Gentiles,
and build up the Church of His blessed Son on
the ruins of their idol temples? Most assuredly
the Lord did not choose us for this high steward-
ship " because we were more in number than
any people,"[1] but (we must believe) that we might
exercise it in His name, and for the accomplish-
ment of His gracious purposes. The history of
the world furnishes no similar instance of a
Christian people brought into such close relations
with a vast Pagan empire. If ever the hand of
God was visible in the government of the world,
it is in the English occupation of India. Surely,
then, it can be no presumption to believe that "a
dispensation of the Gospel is committed to us;"[2]
and if this be admitted, we can hardly refuse to
accept the solemn conclusion of the Apostle—
" Woe unto us if we preach not the Gospel."[3]

The facilities offered to us for the proclamation
of Christ's religion over one great division of
heathendom are greater than were ever afforded

---

[1] Deut. vii. 7.   [2] Gen. ix. 27.   [3] 1 Cor. ix. 16.

to any other Christian nation. For the messengers of His word in India, God may be said to have exalted the valleys and brought low the mountains, thus preparing a highway for them to pass over. Nothing is wanting but more faith and courage, —to go over in reliance upon His promise,—to conquer and possess the land.

But, leaving now this great Asiatic dependency, let us ask what has been the course pursued by the Church towards the various colonies of the British Crown. A short retrospect seems indispensable. It was not till full half a century after the Reformation that England came into possession of her first colony;[G] and when Sir Walter Raleigh landed on the shores of Virginia, it was his tutor, the celebrated Oxford mathematician, Harriot, who was the first to read the Word of God to the wondering Red Indians who flocked round them. It is worth notice, as evidence of the spirit which entered into our earliest colonial enterprises, that when a charter was given by James I. to the Virginia Company, it contained a special provision " that the true word and service of God be preached, " planted, and used, not only in the colonies, but " also among the savages bordering upon them."

Passing on to the period of the Restoration, we find two names dear to history and science—names among the most distinguished that have graced the annals of this University—Clarendon and

Robert Boyle—at the head of a corporation called
" The Society for the Propagation of the Gospel in
New England."[H]   These facts and names are
cited rather in proof of the zeal for the diffusion of
Christianity which animated the early promoters
of colonization, than for any remarkable success
which attended their efforts.

It was not, indeed, till the first year of the 18th
century that any systematic plan for the extension
of the Church in the Colonies was organized.   It
was then—at the instance of some of the most
distinguished Churchmen of the day—that " the
" Society for the Propagation of the Gospel in
" Foreign Parts" received a charter from the hands
of King William III.[I]   Its objects, as therein
defined, are in strict harmony with the spirit of
our Lord's prophetic injunction recorded in the
text, namely, *first* to provide the ministrations of
the Church for the emigrant settlers from our
own shores, and, *secondly*, to preach Christ and His
· salvation to the heathen nations or tribes among
which our countrymen had made their home.

The first and principal field in which the new
Society commenced its labours were the colonies
and plantations on the eastern seaboard of North
America.   Thither were its first missionaries, Keith
and Gordon and Talbot, sent,[K] and there, over
that vast extent of country stretching southwards
from Massachusetts to Georgia, a country at that

time presenting to the eye of the settler little
else than forest, wilderness, and swamp, the first
pioneers of the Gospel laboured in their obscure
spheres of duty, unheard of by the world, and,
for the most part, cut off from intercourse with
each other. Others of like spirit were commis-
sioned from time to time to fill up posts that
death had made vacant, or to occupy new ground;
till at the end of fourscore years a political revolution swept them from the country, and sent
them, like the early disciples at the time of St.
Stephen's martyrdom, to preach the Gospel in other
lands. Was, then, the seed scattered so widely,
and at such a cost, over the rebellious colonies of
America, followed by no harvest? Let the independent and flourishing Church of the United
States, with its 40 bishops and 2,000 clergy,
answer.[L] Let the foundation of the Episcopate—
long and fruitlessly demanded, but at last established in the person of one of the Society's most
honoured missionaries,—answer.[M] Or, better still,
let the answer be sought in that grateful acknow-
ledgment, recorded for all time in the preface to
the Book of Common Prayer, wherein the Church
of America, while preparing to enter upon her
own independent course, confesses herself to be
" indebted under God to the Church of England
" for her first foundation and a long continuance
" of nursing care and protection."[N] To some,

indeed, it may seem like a want of faith to seek
for evidence to prove that "any labour in the
Lord has not been in vain." Still, it is a comfort
and a support to be permitted to see its results;
and on this account we look for our encouragement
to what was accomplished, several generations
since, by the zeal and devotion of a few Churchmen meeting and combining together for the
purpose of extending the Church over the colonies
which had been planted in distant lands, and the
heathen who could be approached through them.
Well may a Church, never left without its cham-
pions and confessors, bless God for His servants,
such as Bray and Wilson and Beveridge and
Patrick and Robert Nelson, who with others
like-minded, in a season of religious apathy and
indifference, laid the foundation of a Society
pledged by its very charter to carry the Gospel
beyond the limits of "Judæa and Samaria, to the
uttermost part of the earth." That Society, though
happy in its standard-bearers, was at the date of
its foundation little known or heeded by the
world at large. Yet it went forth upon its mission
in faith, content to plant and water, as knowing
that God alone could give "the increase." And
so it was that for a whole century that Society
laboured single-handed in the great mission-field
of the Church. For a whole century it was the
solitary witness to the Church's duty of acting

upon her Lord's solemn commission, by going forth in His name and preaching His Gospel in other lands.

But not only was that Society, during the whole of the 18th century, left to struggle on in its arduous work, without any support from state patronage or popular sympathy, it was not even permitted to avail itself of those means of self-government and extension which are the inalienable right, and, indeed, an essential element, of every branch of the Church of Christ. For fourscore years and more, our North American missions, in spite of frequent and urgent remonstrances, were left without a single bishop. For fourscore years every candidate had to come to this country for ordination; for fourscore years no church was consecrated, and no catechumen confirmed. The Church was prevented, by the jealousy of the colonists and the timidity and indifference of the Home Government, from completing her organization; and in this crippled and mutilated condition she remained, till at last a political revolution came to set her free. The close of the last century saw one bishop at Halifax, and another at Quebec.

There, at last, was planted an off-shoot of the heavenly Vine. From that time the Church, no longer an exotic in those regions, began, though slowly, "to take root downward and bear fruit

upward."[1]   Yet how preposterous was even then
the disproportion between the work committed to
the Church, and the instruments with which she
had to execute it! To two bishops were assigned
the oversight and government of our Church, acting
through its feeble and isolated missions, from Newfoundland to Lake Huron; and more than one
generation passed by before any addition was made
to their number.

But at last a time of refreshing arrived. We
may not here trace the successive steps in that
great movement for the full organization of the
colonial Church, to which the first impulse was
given by Bishop BLOMFIELD.[(0)]   Before, however,
his trumpet-call to the Church, some few of the
more glaring deficiencies had been supplied by the
nomination of two bishops for the West Indies, one
for Australia, and two more for North America.
But including these, comparatively recent, additions
to the Episcopate, there were, at the time referred
to, only eight bishops in all for the superintendence
of the Anglican Church in the whole of the colonies
and dependencies of Great Britain.[(1")]
    Come down now, at once, to our own times.
Less than a quarter of a century has elapsed, and
what is the wonderful contrast which is presented
to our sight? The bishops have been multiplied

[1] Isaiah xxxvii. 31.

all but six-fold. Instead of eight there are now forty-seven;[a] the addition to their number within little more than twenty years, being exactly equal to the entire bench of the united Church of England and Ireland put together. But let us endeavour to realize the vastness of the change by a few particular cases.

At the time in question, the whole of Australasia, including Tasmania and New Zealand, was under the spiritual jurisdiction of a single bishop. It is now governed by two metropolitans and eleven suffragan bishops; the several dioceses being, for the most part, fully organized, and all orders in the Church being represented in synods duly convened.[b]

At the same date, the Cape of Good Hope was nominally under the episcopal superintendence of the Bishop of Calcutta. It has since become an ecclesiastical province, with its Metropolitan and suffragan bishops, its synods and missionary conferences. The Church has become a living body, and manifold and wonderful are the tokens of life which its Divine Head has enabled it to manifest to the world.

Must it not, indeed, be regarded as a signal instance of His providential care of the Church, that He has breathed into it this new life just at the moment of our greatest colonial expansion? Profiting by the lessons of a most sad experience in America, the Church, at the epoch more than once alluded to, set herself, for the first time, to accompany her emigrant children to their new homes. Take, as the sufficient examples of this wiser and more consistent course, the two great colonies which have, within our memory, been planted on the Southern Coasts of Australia. The Church may be, almost literally, said to have presided at their foundations. A bishop was sent to MELBOURNE when it was little more than a village, with but three clergymen in the whole province. There are now 100, stationed in all the more important centres of that extensive and prosperous colony, whose population, at present, considerably exceeds half a million, and is increasing by tens of thousands every year. Very similar is the brief history, both of the colony and of the Church, in the neighbouring province of South Australia. One other instance is deserving of especial notice. In the newest British colony—that which only five years ago was planted on the shores of the Pacific —the Church of England accompanied the first settlers, and richly has she been rewarded for her faithfulness by the return to her fold of many who had been estranged, perhaps, by her coldness in times past. [8]

In all these cases, from the very foundation of the new settlements, the Church was present with the earliest colonists, to direct and sanctify their labours, and to remind them "that except the "Lord build the house, their labour is but lost "that build it."[1] But I must abstain from further details, and ask your attention for what remains to some of the more important results of that wonderful extension and organization of the Colonial Church which have distinguished the last quarter of a century. First, then, the foundation of forty new sees, for the most part endowed from private resources, has removed from us the reproach that the Church of England was properly nothing but a child of the State, a mere parliamentary establishment, which had been created and could be abolished by the law ; that it was "an institution as purely local as the Court of Common Pleas ;" well enough adapted to our peculiar habits, but not calculated to bear transplantation, nor vigorous enough to live and flourish under less favourable conditions.[T] It is needless to remind you how triumphantly and for ever this, once popular, objection has been met and answered. But, secondly, the same wonderful extension of the Church, by the settlement of the Episcopate in every quarter of the world, has put to silence the taunt of the Romanist, who had, not so very long since, some plausible grounds for questioning the catholicity of a Church which had never established itself anywhere beyond the

---

[1] Psalm cxxvii.

shores of its own island home. To use any such arguments or objections at the present day, would be to court the readiest refutation. For it would be only necessary to point to the map of the world, and show that there is hardly a country which has been opened to us, by colonization or commerce, where the Church of England is not to be found in the full integrity of its apostolical constitution. Never, then, again shall the taunt of insularity or barrenness be cast against a Church which has her bishops exercising the office and authority, which have descended to them from the Apostles, in India and China, in Ceylon and Borneo, in South and West Africa, in North America from Quebec to Columbia, in the West Indies, in the Islands of the North and South Pacific—a Church, moreover, which, in obedience to her Lord's command, is, at this time, sending out her Missionary Bishops and Priests " to the uttermost part of the earth."

Surely, brethren, a feeling of thankfulness must arise in our hearts as we contemplate the late marvellous growth, and the future altogether unlimited prospects, of our Church ; and good reason have we to say, in the words of the Psalmist, " Thou hast not shut me up into the " hand of the enemy, but hast set my feet in " a large room."[1]

---

[1] Psalm xxxi. 9.

But this great outburst of missionary life has done more than shame into silence the taunts and cavils of jealous rivals on the right hand and on the left. It has quickened our own vital action. It has enlarged our own heart. It has brought into clearer light the true spiritual character of the Church of Christ. It has been the best commentary on the Acts of the Apostles. It has made us feel that we are joined with the first preachers of the Gospel in the commission of our common Lord. It has served to give life and reality to an article of our Creed which was too long, with many, a mere form of words, "*I believe in one Catholic and Apostolic Church*," by making us feel, that not only in the *privileges*, but also in the *obligations* and the *responsibilities* of "the faith" we are *one* with the first disciples.

The same great movement has been fruitful of other blessings still. It has exhibited to us the action of our Church under every variety of new circumstances, and so given proof that it is not dependent on things external.

Has the Church of England been represented as dependent on endowments, and supported by courts of law? Look how firmly she stands, and how freely she moves in Canada and Australia, where she has no foundation but the Rock on which she was originally built, and little provision but what is offered by the love and gratitude of her children.

Have the bishops in this country been assailed by slanderous tongues as owing much of their influence to the peerage and the palace ? See the same apostolic order of men in Newfoundland and New Zealand exercising the same spiritual powers, and regarded with no less reverence, though their houses and establishments are of the humblest character. Again, is it asked how the Church can exist at a distance from ecclesiastical tribunals ? She seems to have found a very tolerable substitute in her own synods, and it may yet be her privilege to show us, by her varied experience in the different colonies, the way to Church-discipline and self-government.

But the glorious onward march of our Church during the last quarter of a century has won for us, and for the true Catholic faith, a more notable triumph than any hitherto named. It has set our "house of defence very high ;" it has, by God's blessing, secured for us a fortress of strength in not fewer than forty commanding positions in every part of the world. These, surely, if any, are buildings of solid and enduring masonry —not "a mere thin coating of Anglicanism," as our work was once somewhat flippantly described.

And goodly, indeed, is the prospect which we are

permitted to contemplate. "Lift up now thine eyes,
" and look from the place where thou art, north-
" ward and southward, and eastward and west-
" ward."[1] Everywhere may be seen the Church
in the perfection of her three-fold ministry, and
firmly based as " a pillar of the truth ; " the centre
of unity to her own children, an abiding witness
for Him who came to be a " Light to lighten the
Gentiles." Thus, then, while contemplating the
solid strength of her foundation, and the breadth
of her extended platform, we may humbly, yet
thankfully, rejoice in the assurance that the Church
which God has long so highly favoured, and of
late so wonderfully extended, is safe under His
protection against the assaults of any foe that may
approach her bulwarks.

Should our own dear Mother be distracted by
heresies, or weakened by fallings-away at home ;
should faith falter, and love grow cold, in this or
that quarter of her horizon, she may re-assure her
heart by casting her eyes abroad, and watching
the heavenly fire burning brightly, as in the first
days of the Church, on the altars which she herself
set up. Let us, then, be no more disturbed by un-
manly and unfaithful fears about the security of our
mother Church. Let us remember it is no longer
the Church of England and Ireland alone—but the
Church of *America*, the Church of *India*, the Church

[1] Gen. xiii. 14.

of *Australia*, the Church of *Africa*. But, brethren, if this reflection should even for a moment awaken in any breast a feeling of national pride, or of self-complacency, let such feeling be at once followed and overpowered by a sense of the fearful responsibility which is thus cast upon us as a nation and a Church. Let us see *what* it is we are called to, by our unequalled opportunities, by our conquests, our colonization, and our commerce. Let us, brethren of the University of Oxford, lay to heart and ponder well the obligation that is laid upon ourselves.

The sermon delivered on the annual recurrence of this holy festival, is proof sufficient that we *acknowledge* our duty to the colonies and dependencies of our empire ; and, if we be sincere, each year ought to find us more zealous and diligent in the *discharge* of it. But, let us pause to ask, is this really the case ? Do we adequately appreciate the value of the ten talents which have been entrusted to us ? Do we seriously consider the account we shall have to render of their use ? The three bishops of India have recently made a united appeal to the universities of England and Ireland. " We call," say they, " in the name of 180 mil-" lions of Hindoos and Mahometans . . . . We " call on Oxford, Cambridge, and Dublin, to send " us more men for Missionary work."—p. 11. Let Oxford be the first to answer that stirring call.

Oxford has piety and learning and wealth. Oxford is a foster-mother of the Church. May not, therefore, Oxford be invited and expected to lead the way in some new and holy league against the Principalities and Powers of Heathendom? Except in some few favoured spots, our great dependency of India is Pagan or Mahometan still. China is all but untouched. Africa has yielded here and there a tribe to the faith of the Gospel, but still remains almost exclusively heathen. Will all these countless millions of our fellow-creatures (some two-thirds of the entire human race) ever be converted to the faith of Christ? We know not. But we know that He who purchased to Himself a universal Church by His own precious blood, gave commandment to His Apostles, and through them to succeeding generations of bishops and pastors, "To go into all the world and preach the Gospel to every creature." We know that, before the end come, "This Gospel of the kingdom shall "be preached in all the world for a witness unto "all nations."[1] We know that all who go forth to teach and baptize in the name of the Holy Trinity, Whom we on this day adore with more especial praise and service, have the promise of their ᐧLord's abiding presence—"Lo, I am with you alway, even unto the end of the world."

Who, then, is ready for the work? Who, when

[1] Matt. xxiv. 14.

the voice of the Lord is heard, "saying, Whom shall I send, and who will go for us?" is ready to answer, *Here I am, send me.* For the pastoral charge of our emigrant countrymen, and for the instruction and evangelization of rude, unlettered savages, men of ordinary gifts—if only their hearts be touched with the love of Christ, and of the souls which He died to redeem—will be found abundantly qualified. But for *India*—we are frequently told and warned—men of learning and intellectual power, men competent to cope with the subtle arguments, and refute the metaphysical fallacies of the more erudite Brahmins, are absolutely required. Has Oxford, of which HEBER and TUCKER and DANIEL WILSON were the honoured representatives in the last generation, and which in more recent times has sent forth MALAN and STREET and FRENCH and KAY—has Oxford none like minded, and as well qualified, to execute their Lord's commission now?

The self-devotion of one such man would be more "than thousands of gold and silver;" and that not one such only, but many such may be found on the rolls of this University it would be painful to doubt. But the responsibility of the Church as a teacher and converter of the Gentiles is too little in our thoughts, and therefore too seldom the subject of our prayers.

This, at least, has been the admitted fault of our

Church in past times. Let us see that it be so no longer. Let us remember that God has not dealt with any modern nation as with our own. Let us bear consciously in mind that through colonization and commerce, through the empire of the ocean, and the almost universal diffusion of our language, He has given to this nation opportunities and openings never accorded to any other.[v] Let us consider, as Christians, that these manifold privileges can have been bestowed upon us for no lower purpose than that of being used for His glory in the extension of the kingdom of His dear Son. Let us seek for faith, that we may rise to the height of His providential designs. Let us desire no honour so much as that of being chosen to be "workers together with Him," for the salvation of a lost world. Let us, for this truly Godlike purpose, be ready to offer ourselves, and all that we hold most dear. Above all, let us make it the subject of our instant and united prayer; let us be like watchmen upon the walls of Jerusalem, who never hold their peace day nor night, who, emboldened and encouraged to plead with the Lord for the fulfilment of His word of promise to the Church, "keep not silence, and give Him no "rest, till He establish and till He make Jerusalem "a praise in the earth."[1]

---

[1] Isaiah lxii. 7.

APPENDIX.

A. p. 6.

THE FOUNDER OF THE RAMSDEN SERMON.

IT is simply an act of justice to put on record a few facts and names connected with the endowment of this sermon. It will be seen, on reference to the *Colonial Church Chronicle*, vol. i. p. 238, that in the year 1847, the necessary means for securing the annual delivery of a sermon, in full term, at St. Mary's, on the extension of the Colonial Church, were placed at the disposal of J. H. MARKLAND, Esq. of Bath, for seventeen years Treasurer, and throughout his whole life a warm supporter, of the *Society for the Propagation of the Gospel.* He handsomely acknowledges that his attention was, in the first instance, directed to that particular scheme by the Bishop of Barbados, then a guest in his house. A similar endowment, at the suggestion of the same excellent Churchman, was obtained for the *University of Cambridge.*

The benevolent founder was a steady supporter of the same Society—an aged lady, " full of good works and almsdeeds," who added to them, as one of the last, the endowment of this sermon—naturally and appropriately called after her name, the " RAMSDEN Sermon."

B. p. 7.

AREA AND POPULATION OF THE BRITISH EMPIRE.

The land area of the earth is 50,000,000 square miles; that of the colonies and dependencies of Great Britain between 8,000,000 and 9,000,000. The total population is computed variously, but taking the mean reckoning of four of the most distinguished geographers, it may be set down at 1,000,000,000, while that of our colonies and dependencies is proximately reckoned at 200,000,000.

C. p. 7.

ENGLISH OCCUPATION OF INDIA.

The English dominion in India may be dated from the victory of Plassey, obtained by Lord Clive over the Hindoos, commanded by Surajah Dowlah, June 23, 1757. A London company of merchants obtained their first charter upwards of a century and a half before—namely, in the year 1600.

D. p. 8.

CHRISTIANS AND MAHOMETANS IN INDIA.

The number of *baptized converts* connected with the missions of the Church of England in *India* (without Ceylon) is somewhat over 60,000, besides a large number under Christian instruction. The native Christians belonging to the missions of other Protestant Communions may be as many, but the number is variously computed.

There is no trustworthy report of the number of Roman Catholic Christians. Mr. Marshall, a very questionable authority, reports them at 1,000,000; more cautious inquirers rate them at about 600,000. It is a striking fact that Queen VICTORIA has more *Mahometan* subjects than the SULTAN.

E. p. S.

BISHOP MIDDLETON'S ARRIVAL IN INDIA.

"No public mark of respect whatever," says Bishop Middleton's biographer, "announced the arrival of the first "Episcopal governor of the Anglo-Indian Church. His "appearance in his diocese was as completely unnoticed by "the authorities as the first landing of a civilian or a cadet."

The Bishop himself, writing to his friend, Mr. Ward, soon after his arrival in Calcutta, says, Dec. 26th, 1814:— " My landing here was without any *eclat*, for fear, I suppose, of alarming the prejudices of the natives." Again, in his letter to the Rev. H. H. Norris, June 3d, 1815, he says :— " My public reception was certainly so arranged as not to "*alarm* the natives. I believe it might *surprise* them, as " they would naturally suppose, considering the high reve- " rence which they pay to the heads of their own religion, " that the arrival of a bishop would make some little stir." —*Le Bas' Life of Middleton*, vol. i. pp. 70, 75, 76.

F. p. 9.

SUB-DIVISION OF BISHOPRIC OF CALCUTTA.

In the preface to his charge to the clergy of the diocese and province of Calcutta (1863), the Bishop most empha- tically records it as his opinion "that the addition of " another member to our Episcopal College would be of the " greatest advantage to the cause of Christianity in India."

This measure had already been pressed upon the attention of Government in a memorial addressed by the Society for the Propagation of the Gospel to the Earl of Aberdeen in 1853. The same subject was a second time brought under the notice of the Government by the Archbishop of Can- terbury in 1856. Again, in the year 1857, the Society— having received urgent applications from most of the prin- cipal stations in the North-West Provinces signed by many persons of eminence, in the civil and military services, including the present distinguished Governor-General, Sir John LAWRENCE—presented a memorial, accompanied by full statistical information, to the Prime Minister, the President of the Board of Control, and the Directors' of the East India Company, humbly praying them " to advise Her Majesty to erect three new Episcopal " sees in India—one at LAHORE for the Punjab, one at

" AGRA for the North-West Provinces, and one at PALAM-
" COTTA for the Province of Tinnevelly ; and also to take
" such steps as may be required for obtaining from Parlia-
" ment the necessary authority for erecting those Sees, as
" well as any others into which Her Majesty may be
" advised, either now or hereafter, to divide the existing
" dioceses of India."

The late Bishop of Calcutta—the venerable Daniel Wilson
—in writing to the Society upon the subject in 1852. uses
these significant words : "If a return to anything like
" primitive Episcopacy could be hoped for, many more
" Sees might be advantageously erected, with small allow-
" ances."

Although the result of the previous efforts for the
increase of the Episcopate in India has been little en-
couraging, it is satisfactory to know that another deputa-
tion, headed by the Primate of England, has very recently
waited upon the Secretary of State for India with the same
object in view, and, let us hope, with better effect.

G. p. 11.

OUR FIRST COLONIES.

NEWFOUNDLAND, indeed, was discovered in 1497 by
Sebastian Cabot, who sailed from the port of Bristol under
the authority of letters patent, granted by King Henry
the Seventh ; but for upwards of a century it was nothing
more than a fishing-station.

VIRGINIA, so named after the virgin Queen Elizabeth,
was taken possession of in 1584 by Sir Walter Raleigh, who,
on assigning over his Patent to a company of merchants,
gave the sum of 100*l*. "in especial regard and zeal of plant-
" ing the Christian religion in those barbarous countries,
" and for the advancement and preferment of the same,
" and the common utility and profit of the inhabitants."
—*Hist. Notices of N. A. Missions*, p. 2. (Bell & Daldy).

H. p. 12.

SOCIETY FOR THE PROPAGATION OF THE GOSPEL IN NEW ENGLAND.

The object of this Society, as defined in its charter, was "not only to seek the outward welfare and prosperity " of those colonies, but more especially to endeavour the " good and salvation of their immortal souls, and the pub- " lishing the most glorious Gospel of Christ among them."

The name of CLARENDON appears first on the list of the Corporators, of which the Hon. ROBERT BOYLE was appointed Governor. The Missionaries were, for the most part, deprived clergymen of the Church of England.— *Hist. Notices*, p. 9.

I. p. 12.

INCORPORATION OF SOCIETY FOR THE PROPAGATION OF THE GOSPEL IN FOREIGN PARTS.

The application for a Royal Charter was strongly supported by the Archbishop of Canterbury (Tenison), and the Bishop of London (Compton). The Charter bears date June 16, 1701.

K. p. 12.

FIRST MISSIONARIES OF SOCIETY FOR THE PROPAGATION OF THE GOSPEL.

The Rev. George Keith (who had been a fellow-student at the University of Aberdeen with Bishop Burnet) and the Rev. Patrick Gordon, embarked for their respective spheres of labour in the *Centurion* on the 24th of April, 1702. The Rev. John Talbot, chaplain of the ship, was so struck with Keith's noble undertaking that he volunteered to join the mission.

D

L. p. 13.

NUMBER OF AMERICAN BISHOPS AND CLERGY.

The total number of American Bishops in 1863 was forty-one, including the Missionary Bishops in China and Siberia, and Bishop Southgate, late of Constantinople. The number of clergy is 2,250.—*Churchman's Calendar.* (New York, 1863.)

M. p. 13.

FOUNDATION OF THE AMERICAN EPISCOPATE.

A few facts may be interesting to the reader. In 1638 Archbishop Laud originated a scheme for sending a Bishop to New England.

A similar proposal was made after the Restoration by Lord Chancellor CLARENDON, who actually obtained from Charles II. a patent for the consecration of Dr. Alexander Murray, as Bishop of Virginia.

Almost immediately after his arrival at New York (1702), the Rev. John Talbot, one of the Society's first Missionaries, strongly urged the necessity of appointing a Bishop for America.

A memorial to the same effect was signed by fourteen clergymen at Boston, in 1705; and one was presented by the Society to Queen Anne, in 1709.

In 1713, another memorial, specifying the need of four Bishops,—one for Williamsburgh, in Virginia; another for Burlington, in New Jersey; and one for each of the islands of Jamaica and Barbados,—was presented to the Queen, and seems to have received the Royal approbation; but, unhappily, the arrangements were put an end to by the Queen's death.

Indeed, the paramount importance of Episcopal super-vision was the constant subject of the letters of the Missionaries; and it was heartily taken up at home by Archbishop Secker, Bishops Sherlock, Butler, Terrick, and Lowth.

But the Episcopate was to be demanded by independent America, before it was conceded to the Colonies of England. For further details the author ventures to refer to a book written by himself nearly twenty years ago—*Historical Notices of North American Missions*, ch. 17.

The Rev. Dr. Samuel Seabury, having served as Catechist for some years, was sent to England for ordination, in 1753. He subsequently occupied different missions of the S.P.G. till 1784, when, having been elected by the clergy of Connecticut, assembled in a voluntary Convention, to be their Bishop, he came once again to England; and was, after some delay, consecrated by the Bishops of the Scotch Church at Aberdeen, on the 14th November, 1784.

Dr. William WHITE and the Rev. Samuel PROVOOST were consecrated Bishops of Pennsylvania and New York, at Lambeth, on the 4th Feb., 1787.

Later in the same year, namely, on the 12th August, Dr. CHARLES INGLIS was consecrated Bishop of Nova Scotia.

N. p. 13.

RATIFICATION OF THE AMERICAN PRAYER-BOOK.

The Book of Common Prayer was ratified "by the " Bishops, the Clergy, and the Laity of the Protestant " Episcopal Church in the United States of America in " Convention," October 16th, 1789.

O. p. 16.

BISHOP BLOMFIELD ON BISHOPRICS FOR THE COLONIES.

The reader is referred to "A Letter from the late Bishop of London to the Archbishop of Canterbury" (Howley), dated April 24, 1840, which is reprinted in *Documents relative to the Erection and Endowment of Additional Bishoprics in the Colonies*, S.P.C.K., 1855. That remarkable letter, after ably developing Bishop Blomfield's plan, concludes with the following striking, almost prophetic words :—

"My own deeply-rooted conviction is, that if the Church of England bestir herself in good earnest, and put forth all the resources and energies which she possesses, and for the use of which she must give account, she will in due time cause the reformed Episcopal Church to be recognised, by all the nations of the earth, as the stronghold of pure religion, and the legitimate dispenser of its means of grace; and will be a chosen instrument in the hands of God for purifying and restoring the other branches of Christ's holy Catholic Church, and of connecting them with herself as members of the same mystical body, in the way of truth, in the unity of the Spirit, and in the bond of peace."

P. p. 16.

BISHOPRICS ERECTED PRIOR TO 1839.

Nova Scotia	1787	Barbados	1824
Quebec	1793	Madras	1835
Calcutta	1814	Australia	1836
Jamaica	1824	Bombay	1837

Q. p. 17.

BISHOPRICS ERECTED WITHIN THE LAST QUARTER OF A CENTURY.

1839—1864.

1 Toronto	1839	6 Guiana	1842
2 Newfoundland	1839	7 Tasmania	1842
3 New Zealand	1841	8 Fredericton	1845
4 Gibraltar	1842	9 Colombo	1845
5 Antigua	1842	10 Capetown	1847

11	Newcastle (Australia) .	1847	29	Columbia .	1859
12	Melbourne . .	1847	30	St. Helena . .	1859
13	Adelaide	1847	31	Nassau (Bahamas) . . .	1861
14	Victoria (Hong Kong) . .	1849	32	Honolulu (Sandwich Is.)	1861
15	Rupert's Land . . . ✝	1849	33	Ontario (Canada) .	1862
16	Montreal . .	1850	34	Goulburn . . .	1862
17	Sierra Leone .	1852			
18	Grahamstown .	1853			
19	Natal	1853		MISSIONARY BISHOPS.	
20	Mauritius	1854			
21	Labuan (Borneo) . .	1855	35	Bishop GOBAT, at Jerusalem	1842
22	Christ Church (N. Zealand)	1856	36	Bishop PATTESON, for Melanesia	1861
23	Perth (Western Australia)	1857	37	Bishop TOZER, Cen. Africa	1861
24	Huron (Canada) . .	1857	38	Bishop TWELLS, Orange River, South Africa .	1863
25	Wellington	1858			
26	Nelson . (New Zealand	1858			
27	Waiapu .	1859	39	Bishop CROWTHER (designate) The Niger . . .	1864
28	Brisbane (Australia) .	1859			

R. p. 17.

PROVINCIAL AND DIOCESAN SYNODS.

In the Colonial and Missionary Church there are at this time five Metropolitan Provinces—namely, Canada, India, Australia, New Zealand, and Capetown. Synods—consisting of the Bishop, the clergy, and lay delegates duly elected—are in full operation in nearly all the dioceses of British North America, of Australasia, and of South Africa.

S. p. 18.

THE CHURCH IN NEW DIOCESES.

The Diocese of MELBOURNE was founded in 1847. At that time the entire population of the colony was 36,000; by the Census of 1861 it had reached 549,901. The number of clergymen was then 3, it is now 100. There was 1 unfinished church, and 2 in course of erection; there were, at the end of 1861, 75 churches, and 3 in progress.

The Diocese of ADELAIDE AND SOUTH AUSTRALIA was founded in 1847, when there were 5 clergymen; in December, 1861, there were 28. The population by the last census (1861) was 126,830.

The colony of BRITISH COLUMBIA was founded in 1858, and was erected into a bishopric in 1859. There are now there a Bishop, Archdeacon, and 14 clergymen.

T. p. 19.

INSULARITY OF THE CHURCH OF ENGLAND.

" The Church of England existed for England alone. It was an institution as purely local as the Court of Common Pleas, and was utterly without any machinery for foreign operations."

" Not a single seminary was established here for the purpose of furnishing a supply of such persons [missionaries and instructors of youth] to foreign countries."— Macaulay; Art. on Ranke's " History of the Popes." *Edin. Rev.*, Oct. 1840.

With regard to the latter observation, it is satisfactory to be able to add, that the Church of England is now happily provided with two very efficient and successful Institutions for the education of missionaries and catechists.

From the Church Missionary Institution, at Islington, founded in 1825, 259 students have been ordained; and from St. Augustine's College, Canterbury, founded in 1848, about 100, who are now labouring in 28 different dioceses.

U. p. 27.

ENGLISH-SPEAKING POPULATIONS.

The population of the 48 *Colonies* of Great Britain is stated, on Government authority, to be 8,666,611 ; from which, if the native races and foreign settlers be deducted, about 5,000,000 will remain who speak the English language —a number equal to the entire population of England in the time of Queen Elizabeth. If this number be added to the population of the United States, estimated in 1860 at 31,429,891, it will be found to be greater by one-fourth than the entire population of the mother country. Moreover, these nations of Englishmen, scattered over every part of the world, are doubling themselves every twenty or twenty-five years; and will, at a very moderate calculation, before the end of the next century, exceed the whole present population of Europe.

THE END.

R. CLAY, SON, AND TAYLOR, PRINTERS, LONDON.

www.ingramcontent.com/pod-product-compliance
Lightning Source LLC
Chambersburg PA
CBHW032138080426
42733CB00008B/1125